Contents

Flowers and Seeds	6
Looking at Flowers	8
Moving Pollen	10
Animal Helpers	12
Flower to Fruit	14
Inside a Fruit	16
All Sorts of Fruit	18
Scattering Seeds	20
Seeds and Animals	22
Waiting to Grow	24
Growing from a Seed	26
Amazing Facts	28
Glossary	29
Index	30

Flowers and Seeds

Most plants have **flowers**.

Flowers grow in lots of different colours, shapes and sizes.

Flowers make a plant's **fruits** and **seeds**. The seeds are inside the fruit.

flower

▶ This is a rose plant. Each flower forms a fruit called a rosehip. Inside the rosehip are the seeds.

rosehip (seeds inside)

Flowers and the seeds they produce are very important. New plants grow from seeds.

◀ A new plant is starting to grow from this seed.

Looking at Flowers

Flowers grow on plants in different ways.

Some plants have one large flower.

▶ A daffodil has one large flower at the top of its **stem**.

Some plants have more than one flower.

◀ This tree has many flowers. We call flowers that grow on trees **blossom**.

Some plants have lots of little flowers held in a single flower head. These tiny flowers are called **florets**.

flower head

florets

petal

△ The yellow centre of each of these flower heads is made up of florets.

Most flowers have **petals**. Petals give the flower shape and colour.

Look at the different flowers on these two pages. What shape and colour are their petals?

Moving Pollen

At the centre of every **flower** are the parts that produce the plant's **fruit**.

▲ You can see the yellow pollen at the centre of this amarylis flower.

Some of these parts make **pollen**. Pollen is a fine powder.

pollen

Look at the centre of different flowers. Can you see the pollen?

Pollen has to move from one flower to another for fruit to form. This is called **pollination**.

Some plants are **pollinated** by the wind. The wind blows pollen from one flower to another.

▲ A hazel bush is pollinated by wind. We call its flowers catkins. Can you see the pollen blowing out of them?

Animal Helpers

Some **flowers** are **pollinated** by animals. These animal helpers are usually insects.

Flowers pollinated by animals make a sugary drink called **nectar**. Many insects feed on this.

When the insect drinks the nectar, **pollen** sticks to its body.

pollen attached to bee

pollen

nectar

Many flowers are brightly coloured and smell sweet. How do you think this helps them to be pollinated?

When the insect goes to another flower to feed, the pollen on its body brushes off on that flower and pollinates it.

◁ Insects move pollen from flower to flower. After this happens, a flower can produce its **seeds**.

In some parts of the world, birds and bats also pollinate flowers.

◁ The hummingbird has a long beak to reach the nectar in the flower.

Flower to Fruit

Once a **flower** is **pollinated** the **fruit** begins to form.

▷ An insect pollinates an apple **blossom**.

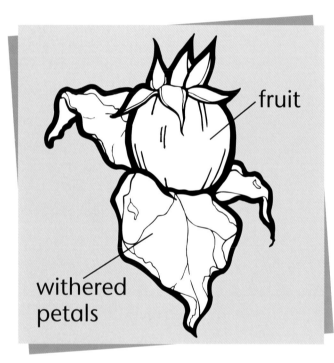

fruit

withered petals

▷ The fruit forms from the centre of the flower. The **petals** drop off, leaving behind a small fruit.

pip (seed)

▲ The fruit grows larger. The plant's **seeds** are inside.

Look at this picture of poppies.

Which part of the flower do you think will become the fruit?

Inside a Fruit

Inside the **fruit** of a plant are its **seeds**. The fruit protects the seeds.

Some fruits hold lots of seeds.

◁ If you cut open a melon, you will find hundreds of seeds.

seed

Some fruits have only a few seeds in them.

▷ Small seeds like grape seeds are often called **pips**.

pip

Some fruits have one seed called a **stone**.

stone

stone

▲ Peaches and avocados have stones.

All the fruit on these two pages are soft and fleshy.

◀ A tomato is a soft and fleshy fruit. We eat the fruit and the seeds inside.

seed

What other fruits do you eat? How many seeds do they have inside them?

All Sorts of Fruit

There are lots of different kinds of **fruit**. Not all of them are soft and fleshy. They all have **seeds**.

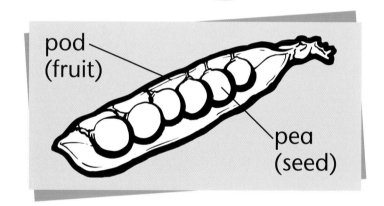

Some seeds form in fruits called **pods**.

▶ Peas are seeds which grow in pods. What other seeds do we eat that come from pods?

pod
(fruit)

pea
(seed)

Some fruits are hard and dry.

◀ An acorn is a dry fruit. Inside its hard shell is a softer seed.

 Do you like eating hazel nuts and peanuts? Nuts are dry fruits. To eat them we crack open the shells and eat the seeds inside.

With some plants, you can't separate the fruits and the seeds. We call these **grains**.

◀ We eat rice and maize grains. We often call maize sweetcorn. ▲

▼ We grind up wheat grains to make flour and then bread.

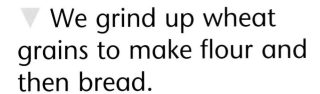

▲ We plant some grains to grow more food. Rice is planted in watery fields called paddy fields.

Scattering Seeds

To grow well, a **seed** needs to move away from the plant that made it. Plants scatter their seeds in different ways.

Some seeds are blown away by the wind.

◀ A dandelion is made up of tiny **florets**. Each one forms a seed with fluffy threads on its top. These float away in the wind.

Have you ever blown a dandelion 'clock'? Try to find one next time you go for a walk. What do the flying seeds remind you of?

Some **pods** dry out on the plant.
They split open and scatter the
seeds inside them on the ground.

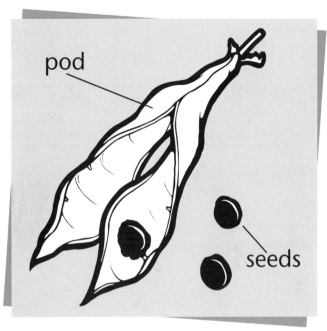

▲ When a lupin pod is dry, it opens
suddenly and the seeds fall out.

Conkers are the seeds of horse chestnut trees.
They grow inside prickly **fruits**, which split
open so the seed inside drops out.

Seeds and Animals

Lots of animals eat **fruits** and the **seeds** inside them. This helps plants spread their seeds.

▶ These mice are eating blackberries, including the hard seeds inside them. After feeding, they will probably move away from the plant.

The seeds inside the fruits pass through the animals that eat them and come out in their droppings.

Birds eat fruit and seeds. Look out for birds feeding when you go for a walk. What are they eating?

Some fruits are light and prickly.
They stick easily to an animal's fur
when it brushes past them.

▲ This is the prickly fruit of a burdock. It is called a **burr**.

▲ Burrs hook themselves to an animal's coat when it brushes past them

Later the fruits drop off the animal and the seeds inside can begin to grow.

Has a burr ever stuck to you, or maybe to your pet cat or dog?

Waiting to Grow

Seeds may lie in the ground for a while. They need water and warmth to start to grow.

In parts of the world where there are cold winters, seeds start to grow in the spring when the weather is warmer.

◄ A farmer sowed this wheat in the winter. Now it is spring, the wheat has started to grow.

► Some gardeners help seeds to grow by keeping them warm inside greenhouses.

In the desert there is very little rain.
Seeds lie in the ground for a long time
and grow very quickly after it rains.

▲ After a rainstorm in the Australian desert, plants
grow and flower quickly to make more seeds.

Try growing some seeds such as cress or
mung beans on a sunny window sill. Give
some of them water. Keep some of them dry.
Which ones start to grow?

Growing from a Seed

Inside every **seed** is the beginnings of a new plant. It is protected by the seed's case until it starts to grow.

sunflower seed

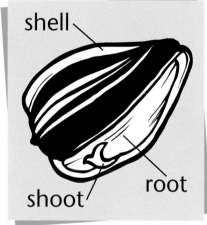

shell

shoot

root

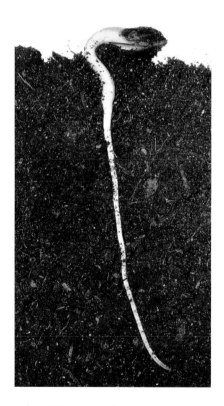

▲ Inside a seed is a **root** and a **shoot**. There is also a store of food to give the new plant the energy it needs to start growing.

▲ First the root begins to grow down into the ground.

▲ Then the shoot pushes up above the ground and open its **leaves**.

Try growing some beans. Soak the beans in water overnight and push them down the side of a glass jar filled with damp cotton wool. Put the jar somewhere sunny. Over the next week, watch as the root and the shoot start to grow.

▲ A plant makes food in its leaves. This gives it the energy to grow bigger and **flower**.

▲ Insects visit the flower to feed on the **nectar** it makes. They **pollinate** the plant.

▲ The **petals** die. The plant has made its **fruits** and seeds – so more new plants can grow.

Amazing Facts

The largest flower is the stinking corpse lily. The flower is found in Asia and measures about 91cm (36 inches) across.

A honeybee visits between 50 and 100 flowers on every trip it makes from its hive to collect nectar for making honey. Think how many flowers it helps pollinate during its lifetime!

The largest seed is the coconut. The double coconut found in the Seychelles in the Indian Ocean weighs 18kg, about as much as a small child.

Use your book to find the answers to this Amazing Plants quiz!

- What is a floret?

- How does pollen travel from one plant to another?

- Once a flower has been pollinated, what happens to its petals?

- How do we eat wheat grains?

- Name three fruits that have stones inside them.

- How do animals help plants by eating their fruit?

- Is a pod a flower, a fruit or a seed?

28

Glossary

blossom flowers that grow on trees.

burr a type of prickly fruit that sticks to hair, fur or clothing.

floret a small flower that is part of a bigger flower head.

flower part of a flowering plant that makes its fruits and seeds. Flowers are often very colourful.

fruit part of a plant that grows from the flower and protects the seed or seeds.

grains the seeds made by cereal plants such as wheat and rice. We eat a lot of grains.

leaf part of a plant that is usually green. The leaf uses sunlight, air and water to make food for the plant.

nectar a sugary liquid made in some flowers as food for insects and other animals. These feeding animals pollinate the flowers as they move between plants.

petals outer parts of a flower that are often colourful.

pips small, hard seeds found in some fruits.

pod a type of fruit that grows on some plants, such as bean and pea plants.

pollen a fine powder made by flowers.

pollinated see **pollination**.

pollination the movement of pollen from one flower to another. Flowers need to be pollinated to form their fruits and seeds. Pollen is moved from plant to plant by the wind or by animals.

root part of a plant that holds the plant in the soil. The roots take up water from the soil.

seed seeds are made in the flower of a flowering plant. When seeds are planted new plants grow from them.

shoot the first growth of a plant above the ground made up from a stem and a leaf or two leaves.

stem part of a plant that holds up the leaves and flowers and connects with its roots.

stone a large, single hard seed found in some fruits like plums, peaches and nectarines.

Index

acorn 18
amarylis 10
animals 12, 22, 23
avocados 17

beans 27
   mung 25
blackberries 22
blossom 8, 14

catkins 11
conker 21
cress 25

daffodil 8
dandelion 20
desert 25

energy 26, 27

florets 9, 20
flour 19
food 27
fruit 7, 10, 14, 15, 16, 18, 19, 27

grains 19
grapes 16
greenhouses 24

hazel 11, 19
horse chestnut 21
hummingbird 13

insects 12, 13, 14, 27

leaves 26, 27

lupin 21

maize 19
melon 16

nectar 12, 13, 27
nuts 19

paddy fields 19
peaches 17
peanuts 19
peas 18
petals 9, 14, 27
pips 15, 16
pods 18, 21
pollen 10, 11, 12, 13
pollinated 11, 12, 13, 27
pollination 10
   animal 12, 13, 27
   wind 11
poppies 15

rice 19
root 26
rose 7
rosehip 7

shoot 26
spring 24
stem 8

tomato 17

wheat 19, 24
wind 11, 20
winter 24